Solstice

Zinnie Harris's plays include the multi-award-winning *Further than the Furthest Thing*, produced by the National Theatre/Tron Theatre in 2000 (1999 Peggy Ramsay Playwriting Award, 2001 John Whiting Award, Edinburgh Festival Fringe First award); *Nightingale and Chase* (Royal Court Theatre, 2001); *By Many Wounds* (Hampstead Theatre, 1999); and *Silver Whale Fish* and *Master of the House* (BBC Radio Four). *Solstice* is the first in a trilogy of plays, of which the second, *Midwinter*, was staged by the RSC in 2004, and the last, *Fall*, awaits completion. Zinnie Harris was recently awarded an Arts Foundation Fellowship for playwriting, and was Writer in Residence at the RSC, 2000–2001.

ZINNIE HARRIS

Solstice

ff

faber and faber

First published in 2005
by Faber and Faber Limited
3 Queen Square London WC1N 3AU

Typeset by Country Setting, Kingsdown, Kent CT14 8ES
Printed in England by Mackays of Chatham plc, Chatham, Kent

A CIP record for this book
is available from the British Library

ISBN 0–571–22919–0

2 4 6 8 10 9 7 5 3 1

Solstice was first performed by the Royal Shakespeare Company at The Other Place, Stratford-upon-Avon, on 30 March 2005. The cast was as follows:

Michel Peter Bygott
Sol Eke Chukwu
Thomas Neil McKinven
Adie Alan Morrissey
Jean Kevin Trainor
Therese Suzanne Burden
Hannah Frances Jeater
Sita Sally Tatum

Flutes Max Gittings

Directed by Zinnie Harris
Designed by Tom Piper
Lighting designed by Phil Ash
Sound designed by Tim Oliver
Music composed by John Harris
Movement directed by Liz Ranken
Company voice work by Jan Haydn Rowles

Characters

Adie

Sita

Michel

Therese

Thomas

Hannah

Sol

Jean

Authors Note

Solstice is the first in a trilogy of plays,
Solstice, *Midwinter* and *Fall*.

Solstice takes place ten years before *Midwinter*.

SOLSTICE

Act One

Sita and Adie, two young people, snogging.

Sita
You ever pause for breath?

Adie
no, you?

Sita
ow

Adie
what?

Sita
that hurt

Adie
what did?

Sita
your knee it caught my –

Adie
sorry

Sita
you got a fag?

Adie
later

Sita
no now.

Adie leans back.

Adie
You shouldn't smoke

Sita
lots I shouldn't do. You going to give me one or what?

Adie shrugs.
He gets one out.

Sita
I thought you said you didn't smoke?

Adie
I don't

She takes one.

Adie
do you want to lie down or something?

Sita
what to smoke my fag?

Adie
no I mean . . .

She laughs.

Adie
what?

She laughs more.
Adie blushes.

Sita
You should shave by the way

Adie
I do shave

Sita
shave better then. Use a proper razor or something.
I bet I will have zits in the morning

Adie
you'll still look beautiful to me

She lights the fag.
She smokes it.
He kisses her again.
She kisses him.

Sita
you taking the piss?

Adie
no

Sita
better not be

Adie
I wasn't.

She smokes her fag.

Sita
What is this place anyway?

Adie
just a place I come to

Sita
what sort of place?

Adie
I don't know

Sita
it looks like a chapel

Adie
nah

Sita
a prison then

5

Adie

    I don't think so.
    It was a house that never got built

Sita

    maybe it was a brothel

Adie

    maybe it was.

Sita

    You ever sleep here?

Adie

    sometimes

Sita

    where?

Adie

    curl up over there

Sita

    the rain doesn't get you?

Adie

    no

She curls up.
She looks up to the ceiling.

Sita

    get away
    you never slept here
    you'd be soaked right through

Adie

    I come here to think

Sita

    oh yeah, about what?

Adie

    stuff

Sita
  right

Adie
  don't laugh

Sita
  I wasn't laughing.
  sometimes I think you might be about ten

Adie
  fuck off

Sita
  well it is a kiddie thing isn't it,
  Saying you go places to think
  It is like having a den or sitting in your treehouse

Adie
  I am the same age as you

Sita
  yeah but I am out there.
  I have seen things
  I don't say I go places to think.

Adie
  I keep a gun here

Sita
  you do not

Pause.

Adie
  show you if you like

Sita
  whatever

He goes to a little box.
He gets out a gun.
He aims it at her.

Sita
  fucking hell

Adie
  I told you

Sita
  well point it the other way

Adie
  why?

Sita
  Adie

He holds it right up to her face.
Then makes a line across her body.
She doesn't move.
He throws it on the ground.
He laughs.
Pause.

Sita
  that wasn't funny

Adie
  so don't laugh

Sita
  I thought we came here to shag I didn't think you were going to aim a flipping gun at me

Adie
  it isn't even loaded

She looks at it.
She touches it with her foot.

Sita
  why have you got it then?

Adie shrugs.

Adie
  It doesn't even work, rusted over
  Only a woman would be scared

She picks it up.
Pause.

Sita
  can I keep it?

Adie
  why?

Sita
  just for a day
  just overnight
  just so that if I am scared I can . . .

She aims it.

Adie
  it doesn't work I told you

Sita
  please

Adie
  who are you scared of?

Sita
  never you mind

Adie
  maybe I could help you

Sita
  sure
  Maybe you could

Pause.

Sita
  after you've done everything else
  After you've studied a bit

9

And got your exams. And had the summer holiday
Its okay I don't mind.
Listen I like you.
I watch you.
I see you coming out of the school
I wait for you with my line of sight
I follow you with my hand all the way home
you haven't seen me?

Adie
no

Sita
well look next time
high up
Where you can see everything
Who you talk to
What you are wearing
If you stop to do up your shoelace on your way out of
the gates

Adie
are you stalking me?

Sita
I like you I told you.

Beat.

Sita
or I did before you aimed a gun at me.

Adie
I saw the bride.
I saw her getting done.

Beat.

Adie
I was like you, I was watching
Only I was below

    They were on the bridge
    I was on the bank

Sita
    you didn't do anything?

Adie
    what could I do?

Beat.

Adie
    I thought you liked me

Sita
    I do

Adie
    then tell me what I could have done.

Beat.

Sita
    I don't know.
    Don't ask me.
    I'm not the person to ask about this.

Adie
    she didn't have a chance
    He got her in a stranglehold before she could even yell

Sita
    I don't want to hear

Adie
    and this knife.
    This bloody great knife

Sita
    Adie.

Beat.

Adie

I should have broken his neck.

Sita

you are just a kid.

Adie

I am the same age as you.

Sita

yeah but what could I have done?

Adie

I fucked it

Sita

who knows?

Adie

I saw her body stop moving.
I saw her face go grey when all the blood left it.
I saw him take the skin off her like she was a rabbit.

Sita

I don't want to hear okay

Sita comes over and kisses him.
Adie breaks away.

Adie

give me the gun back

Sita gives him the gun back.
He puts it back in the cubby hole.

Adie

it belongs here.

Sita

You've got to forget it,
that is what we all have to do.
You have to think, right that happened,

Now it is gone.
You can't screw up the rest of your life because of this.
We all have things like this.
So you grew up that day.
Big deal.
We all have to grow up.
Kiss me.
That is what we came here for isn't it?

They kiss.

Sita
No one saves anyone.
Everyone thinks what they would have done
afterwards.
Every one runs,
That is the truth.
Every single person runs.
You are just human, you just save your own skin.

He shows his hand to her.

Adie
I drove a nail into my hand.
While I watched.

She looks.
She doesn't make any response.

Adie
I haven't cleaned it

Beat.

Sita
you are lucky.
You are a really lucky kid.
You should hang on to that

Adie
you don't know that

Sita
yes I do.

She starts to unbutton her blouse.
She takes her shirt off.
Her chest is horribly scarred.
Pause.

Sita
This is what happens if you don't run

Beat.

Sita
or you can't run
or you just aren't fast enough

Beat.
Sita starts to button up again.

Adie
show me again

Sita
no fear

Adie
it's beautiful

Sita
you wanker

Adie
I love you

Sita
you don't need to say that

Adie
let me look again

She puts her shirt back on.

Sita
    no

Adie
    who did it?

Sita
    They didn't tell me their names.
    Funnily enough.
    Anyway what are you going to do, chase after them
    for me?

Sita laughs.

Adie
    don't laugh

She laughs harder.

Adie
    I said stop it

Sita
    I'm only joking

Adie
    shut up

Sita
    it's funny

Adie
    I said shut up.

He pushes her away.

Sita
    Okay.
    You don't need to push me.
    I get the message.

Pause.

Sita
I am not going to beg you Adie
I thought you and I could be friends.
I thought we might have a laugh.
I don't want this from you
I don't want to sit here and have a heavy discussion
I don't want to get depressed thinking about shit
things.

She picks up her bag.

Sita
I'll see you yeah?

Adie
don't go.

Sita
just forget it

Adie
Sita?

She has gone.
Adie is left alone in the hideout.

SCENE TWO

A little room in a poor house.
The wallpaper is peeling from the walls. The light is dim.
Michel and Therese, both in their fifties, come back in.
Michel puts on the light.

Therese
Thirty-two

Michel
at least seventeen

Therese
you say that about everyone

16

Michel

I say everyone under twenty, but him –

Therese

twenty-five if he was a day

Michel

you said thirty a minute ago

Therese

a little difficult to age, perhaps but well over twenty

He laughs.

Michel

anyway it is just a sign of ageing I expect. When I am another ten years older the world will look like it is run by toddlers

Therese

it is.

Pause.

Michel

I liked him as a matter of fact

Therese

did you?

Michel

a little clean-shaven perhaps, a little green about the gills but –

Therese

he has a lisp

Michel

the good lord will forgive a lisp

Therese

yes but will the congregation?

Michel laughs.

Michel
the cruthifithion of Chritht.

He laughs again.

Michel
We will organise a whip-round. A little speech therapy.
If he is to stay we will need to be able to hear him

Therese
It's his teeth

Michel
nothing wrong with his teeth

Therese
the top tooth, like an obtrusion, it got in the way

Michel
you're too harsh.
You should judge him by what he says not the way he
says it

Therese
I would if I could have understood it.

Michel laughs.
He puts his arms around her.
Beat.

Michel
Let's go on a walk tonight.
Let's forget the meal
Let's stroll out like we used to

Therese
tonight

Michel
make each other laugh.
It's so hot in this house, the air

Therese
  I am already going out tonight

Beat.

Therese
  you know that.
  The women

Michel
  of course

Therese
  they are expecting me

Michel
  the dice

Therese
  one night a week
  the other six

Michel
  we'll do it another night

Therese
  tomorrow

Michel
  yes

Therese
  I'd like that.
  We don't walk as much as we used to,
  we don't talk

Michel
  we talk all the time

Therese
  we don't always listen, we don't always laugh

Michel
we are like any couple then
after so long

Therese
probably.

Pause.

Michel
Another night then.
Abandon the evening ritual
the chipping of wax, the evening meal
do something for ourselves.
They are opening up some of the old roads again.
We could stroll over to the woods

Therese
we would be bitten to death

Michel
we could bite each other

Beat.

Therese
okay

Michel
okay.

Beat.

Michel
you are probably right, the insects at this time of year.
In this heat

Therese
we could take a picnic

Michel
yes we could

Beat.

Michel

it's a long time since we have walked up there

Therese

they are building an airfield
it's only open to the military.
You get too near, you get shot.

Michel nods.

Michel

I suppose they need a place to put all these planes they
have now.

Therese

I won't be long
A quick game with the women
half an hour

Beat.

Michel

one day you must explain the attraction of dice.
Yes?
Me I don't see it.
I try but –
So you roll one number, then you roll another.
That is it

Therese

it's more complicated

Michel

but in essence
it is one number or another

Therese

I suppose

Michel

and yet the pull is enormous

Therese
  dice isn't an evil Michel

Michel
  I know

Therese
  you make it sound like it's a vice

Michel
  no no

Therese
  I haven't read anywhere that dice is wrong

Michel
  I suppose it might be like eating liquorice after wine.
  The two so soon
  it is either to your taste or not.

Therese
  I like to go out Michel.
  That is all
  god I spend long enough in.
  In the evenings
  I feel like I can breathe better in the evening
  when the heat has passed

She stops.
She breathes sharply.
She holds her breath.
She waits until it passes.

Therese
  A stitch that is all
  I spoke too loud

Michel
  you should eat something

Therese
  they will be food there

Michel
  unnutritious food that Hannah cooks.
  No wonder you are losing weight

She kisses him on the top of his forehead.

Therese
  I have stopped listening.

Michel
  So you have.

Beat.
She has gone.
He gets out a bottle of wine.

Michel
  So you have.

It feels a bit sour. And a bit lonely.
He picks up the paper.
He throws it down.
The light starts to go.
He goes over to it and thumps it.
It comes back on, then goes off again.

Michel
  Damn.

He gets out a candle.
He lights it.
There is a knock at the door.

Michel
  Changed your mind
  or lost the game already
  don't tell me
  walking down the road and thought to yourself
  I miss his company
  Do you know what? I miss that old fool
  He might drive me crazy and every one might have

warned me off him, but do you know what? I miss the
daft old man

Thomas
Michel.

Michel turns around.

Michel
Well you will have to step in, I can't see you in this
blessed light.

He takes the candle over to the door.

Michel
Well well

Thomas
I tried to phone

Michel
it doesn't work

Thomas
I gathered

Michel
it works on Mondays generally, but the rest of the
week

Thomas
it was a Thursday.

Michel
Nah.
Never try to do anything on a Thursday
and the light, don't ask me about the light. Normally
we have good light but today, just a moment ago –

Thomas
maybe a loose connection

Michel
maybe

Beat.

Michel
so you are returned

Thomas
only briefly

Pause.

Michel
well come in come in, I'll get another candle.

He gets another one out and lights it.

Michel
it is the right era to be a candlemaker Thomas, I tell
you that. You might think bread is the future, but
candles, when the electricity is as bad as it is.
Sometimes I think it is like my private angel, the more
it goes wrong the more I sell.

He lights a third.
And a fourth.

Michel
And now we have more candles than we can hold.
Thank you Mr National Grid

Thomas comes in.

Michel
Your face
your face has changed do you know that?
all our faces change but yours

Thomas
exactly the same

Michel
no a little wiser now, is that it? Have you got wise?
You still make bread?

Thomas
Of course

Michel
You still make the bread with currants in it?

Thomas
The very same.

Michel
And the buns with the holes?

Thomas
Doughnuts

Michel
very good

Thomas
I have some in the car

Michel
because Therese –
she needs feeding.

Thomas
I'll bring them in.

Michel
A car, did you say you had a car?

Thomas
parked outside

Michel
but the mud

Thomas
I put bags under the wheels

Michel laughs.

Michel
the same as the military then
wine?

Thomas
of course

Michel
and the business, the business is good?

Thomas
yes

Michel
you still stamp the bread?

Thomas
not so much

Michel
oh?

Thomas
there is not so much need for it as there was

Michel
you don't stamp the bread

Thomas
sometimes I stamp it, of course sometimes I stamp it
but other times
you know how it is

Michel
you don't stamp it

Thomas
not so much.

Michel pours him some wine.

Thomas
Thank you
where is Therese anyway?

Michel
dice game.
You could run and catch her but –

Thomas
it is you I want to talk to anyway

Michel
me?

The light flickers.
It comes back on, briefly.

Michel
Tell me is the electricity the same the city over?

Thomas
we don't experience quite these problems

Michel
no?

Thomas
no, and the telephone works

Michel
does it really?

Thomas
you pick it up, dial and there you are

Michel
amazing

The light comes back on.
Beat.

Michel
would you look at that.
The very invention of it.

Doesn't it just blow your mind.
The light bulb is something. Something out of the
ordinary.

Thomas
it isn't a new invention

Michel
it still is worth celebrating.
Every time the electricity comes back on I am amazed.

Thomas
You must spend your life amazed.

Michel
You would think wouldn't you?

Beat.

Thomas
How is Adie?

Michel
We think he should do well
he studies
the teachers speak highly of him

Thomas
that is good.

Beat.

Michel
Have you any thought to see your mother while you
are here?

Thomas
Therese said she doesn't recognise anyone

Beat.

Thomas
I'll pop in.

Michel
You never mention her.

Thomas
I'll pop in.

Pause.

Thomas
I always forget what the inside of your house looks like
you know that
I feel like I know the outside better
from sitting on hot evenings

Michel
what is wrong with the inside?

Thomas
nothing
a few too many pictures for my liking

Michel
icons

Thomas
staring faces

Michel laughs.

Michel
they are supposed to bring comfort

Thomas
to the sick perhaps
the very sick.

Michel laughs again.

Michel
Why are you here Thomas?

Thomas
I have a very large house

Michel

you have come to tell me you have a large house?

Beat.

Thomas

Two storeys. And a garden

Michel

is that so?

Thomas

all this space and just me

Michel

maybe if you took a dog you'd have less space
you need a dog to run in the garden, is that it?

Beat.

Thomas

the land is sinking

Michel

no

Thomas

you have to put polythene under your car in the street

Michel

luckily not that many of us have cars
the land is sinking yes, but not as fast as they will tell
you
not tomorrow fast, or even this time next year fast
the house will still be here when Adie is the same age
as me.
A hundred years from now, this house will still be
standing.
And here they still stamp the bread, we like that.

Beat.

Thomas
Do you think I wasn't nervous about moving when I
first went?

Michel
I don't remember you putting up a resistance

Thomas
I went because I saw sense

Michel
you saw a living

Thomas
and what is wrong with that?
Money is not the great evil Michel

Michel
I know

Thomas
I saw a chance of making a little money yes, drinking
water that doesn't taste of your neighbours' pee,
stepping outside and not encountering a swamp

Michel
it is not a swamp

Thomas
and the flies
I don't know how you put up with the flies.

Pause.
Michel drinks his wine.
Beat.

Thomas
I am not saying everything about the city is easy.
I'm not saying it is ideal but . . .
It is better than here.

Beat.

32

Michel
    Did Therese ask you to talk to me?

Thomas
    I have never mentioned it to her.
    It must have occurred to her, but I have never said

Michel
    then please don't
    we will say nothing of this conversation

Pause.

Michel
    I have good friends on the other side of the river, I am
    not saying I have anything against it, but for me, for
    us. No.

Thomas
    She is a very loyal woman Michel

Michel
    she is your sister, of course you would call her loyal.
    You don't have a wife and child but if you did –

Thomas
    what is there for them here?

Michel
    there is me
    it might not seem like much to you. But there is me.

Beat.

Michel
    Don't let's argue
    you are here for such a short time.
    We are fine.
    You don't know how fine we are.

He pours him more wine.

Thomas
And when you stop being fine?

Michel
Who knows?
Who knows what any of us would do when we stop
being fine?

Thomas
I'd forgotten how stubborn you are

Michel
then it has been too long since you have seen us.

Thomas
Michel can I be honest with you?

Michel
Of course.

Thomas
You don't have a choice

Michel
I am sorry

Thomas
I am offering you a lifeline.
I . . .
I shouldn't tell you this, but as I know
How can I not tell you?
I am a businessman, yes.
And business men, we get together.
We tell each other things.
There is a fair exchange of communication you could
say

Michel
what are you on about?

34

Thomas
you are all going to be moved
bulldozed.
The plans are already on the wall.
There is no possibility of staying here beyond the end
of the year

Michel
I don't understand you

Thomas
if you were smart you would move now
they want the land

Michel
they want this stinking swamp?

Thomas
I suppose so

Michel
if that were true someone would have told us

Thomas
I am telling you now

Michel
they would have put it in a newspaper or something

Thomas
and start a war?

Beat.

Thomas
there is bad enough feeling.
Of course they aren't going to tell you.
They are hoping that enough will move of their own
accord.
The mud is getting worse.
The electricity.

The place is falling apart. I expect they hope that
people will leave because they can't cope with it any
more.
Already they are building that airfield to fly in the
machines that will knock down your houses.
You are my family.
Your neighbours are my neighbours.
I came from here.
I am only telling you what I know before you have run
out of time to do anything about it.
You have to come and live with me.
All of you.
You don't have any choice.
I am sorry but that is the way it is.

Michel

I have friends in the city. I send candles every week.
Are you asking me to believe this of my friends?

Thomas shrugs.

Thomas

Don't ask me.
How do I know what happens in a man's conscience?
This bride, it has changed the landscape. The feeling
isn't the same. And they want your land

Michel

this isn't land, it's mud

Thomas

they want the mud then

Michel

they want the mud?

Thomas

under the mud

Michel

dead fish

36

Thomas
well under the dead fish then.
I don't know, something they want to mine

Michel
they want to mine our mud?

Thomas
yes

Michel
this mud that has cursed us?

Thomas
you said it hadn't

Michel
this mud that has got into our chests, our lungs,
between our toes, into our children's eyes?

Thomas
yes

Michel laughs.

Thomas
it's not funny

He laughs again.

Thomas
it isn't funny

Michel
it is so funny I could wet myself
It is so funny I feel like I might shit my pants
the mud turns out to be valuable, and you tell me that
isn't funny

Thomas sighs.

Thomas
I wish you would take this seriously

Michel

how can I when you come and tell me jokes?

Thomas

I can take you up to the town hall. Talk to the man
that I talked to.
He'll tell you what he knows.
Even the people I sell bread to, they all know.
It is common knowledge over there

Michel

but not over here it seems.

Thomas

Walk up the old road
go to the airfield
see the machines they are bringing in
they will move you Michel
and if you leave it until you are bulldozed what else
will there be?

Pause.

Michel

I have friends on the other side of the river Thomas
Good friends, friends who would do a thing or two for
me.
I am popular over there.
The people I sell my candles to
They like me. We have a joke.
Now are you telling me that they are going to stand by
and do nothing?
I cannot believe this of my friends.
I cannot believe if they knew this they wouldn't tell me.

Thomas shrugs.
Pause.

Michel

I may not be a great thinker Thomas
I may not live in a place with schools that have tennis
courts
But I know how things are
And I know how friendship works.

Pause.

Thomas

Then you'll see my coming here was the gesture of a
friend.

Thomas puts the wine down.

Michel

Finish the wine with me.

Thomas

I have to get back.

He puts his hand out.

Thomas

I broke all kinds of codes telling you.
Codes that would cost me my friends.

Michel

What about the others?
They will want to see you.
What about the rest of your family?

Thomas

Don't be too stubborn Michel.

He kisses him.
And leaves.

SCENE THREE

Therese throws dice.
She is alone.
She doesn't like the number.
She throws again.
She feels faint.
She sits down.
She takes out a handkerchief and wipes her brow.
She retches a couple of times.
She picks up her dice.
She breathes on them.
She throws them again.
She looks.
Sita is sitting close by. Therese notices.

Therese
    You don't need to watch me
    I don't need an audience.
    I am just getting up I just –

Sita puts out a hand.

Therese
    I have a headache, I just need it to pass

Beat.

Therese
    you don't need to, I'm fine.

Hannah, a woman in her sixties, enters.

Hannah
    She is with me.

Sita
    she looks sick

Therese
I felt a little faint

Hannah
she will be okay

Sita
she shouldn't be in the street late at night

Hannah
neither should you.

Sita
I am invisible.
Trouble passes me by.

Hannah
You look like a trouble magnet to me.

Sita
Why did you say that? You didn't need to say that.
I am just helping your friend

Beat.

Hannah
sorry.

Sita
She has got two sixes

Therese
have I?

Therese looks at the dice.

Sita
must have some luck somewhere.

Sita goes.

Hannah
You didn't come to the game

Therese
  I tried
  I . . .
  I found I needed to sit
  So I sat.

Hannah
  Are you sick?

She looks at the dice.

Therese
  You heard the girl. I just rolled two sixes, how can I be
  sick?

Hannah laughs.

Therese
  Do you pray Hannah?
  I mean really pray.
  Get down on your knees and really . . .

Hannah
  Sometimes

Therese
  I used to pray

Hannah
  good

Therese
  I don't any more
  I go through the motions
  I try
  I hold my breath
  I recite prayers

Hannah
  it doesn't matter

Therese
  it should matter

Even in the slide of my mother's own dementia prayers
were the last to go.
If she could say the words why can't I?
I can't even use the word 'God' any more
I say the word
I want to laugh.
I know that sounds stupid but –

Hannah
everyone goes through this.

Therese
And the host.
There is all the fuss about which way the host is
walked
around the church.
People have fought and died
I see the host
I think you are a tiny piece of bread.
That's all.
I am going to eat you
I am going to chew you into a thousand pieces.
You crumb.

Hannah laughs.

Therese
Don't.

Hannah
It's funny

Therese
it's not funny

Hannah
you said it to make me laugh.

Therese
I didn't.

And in church when everyone is silent
I want to scream.
I want to scream out what is all this nonsense about?
Why does it raise such animosity?
It's just a piece of bread.
A church should not be founded on the direction that
a piece of bread is marched.

Hannah
You should shout it

Therese
I would be mown down.

Hannah
People would think you were crazy but you would
have said it

Therese
I'd be locked up

Hannah
God would forgive you.

Therese
Don't say that
It doesn't help.
I told you, I can't even hear the word these days
I wish I could say that, like you did
I wish I could have the certainty that you have.
You are like Michel, you and he

Hannah
I'm not as bad as Michel.

Beat.

Therese
No.

Beat.
Therese picks up the dice. She plays with them in her hand.

Therese
Yes, I'm sick.

Pause.

Therese
You asked the question
That is the answer.

Hannah
How sick?

Therese
I get a sensation.
It can start at any time, no warning
this feeling that my bones are being crushed very
slowly

Hannah
it's a migraine

Therese
it's all over my body

Hannah
you take wintergreen?

Therese
I chew wintergreen like there was no tomorrow
but even the wintergreen –
Michel says I have lost weight.

Hannah looks at her.

Hannah
And have you?

Therese
I don't know

Hannah
we all lose weight in the summer

Therese
that is what I told him

Hannah
do you eat properly?

Therese
Sometimes
maybe it is the wintergreen, maybe it affects my appetite
maybe I shouldn't take so much
but then the sensation –

She throws the dice again.

Hannah
What does the doctor say?

Therese
not much

Hannah
there you are then.
He isn't worried.
He is a good doctor, if he was worried he would have
plenty to say

Hannah goes into her pocket.
She pulls out a bar of chocolate.

Hannah
Have some chocolate
And don't ask me where I got it

She gives it to Therese.

Therese
what would happen to Adie?

Hannah
what do you mean?

Therese
what would happen to Adie?
without me?

Beat.

Hannah
There isn't going to be any without you
I will bring chocolate to your door every morning if
I have to.

Therese
I haven't bled.
Months now

Hannah
it is the menopause there you are
we all get weird symptoms with the menopause.

Therese
I thought maybe there was a baby.
That was the bloating.
My stomach is swollen.
It is rock-solid.
There is something there.
It doesn't move.
It doesn't kick.

Beat.

Therese
Give me your hand.

Hannah gives her her hand.
Therese puts it on her stomach.

Therese
Don't tell me that is the menopause.
And don't tell me that means life.

Pause.

47

Therese
Michel can be so distant with Adie

Hannah
don't worry

Therese
the two of them they –

Hannah
he loves that boy
I can see he loves that boy. We all love that boy.

Therese cries a little.

Hannah
Don't cry.
Oh cruel God.
Don't cry.
Hey, sweetheart. Don't cry.

SCENE FOUR

Michel is sitting brooding on the front step.
Adie comes back.

Michel
Bit late for you isn't it?

Adie
bit late for you.

Beat.

Michel
where have you been?

Adie shrugs.

Michel
I have seen you hanging around that old building.

48

Adie

So?

Michel

All kinds of people use it.
I think you should know that.

Beat.

Adie

You've got a package

Michel

oh

Adie

it was left on the doorstep

He gives it to Michel.

Michel

it is from my friends.
There we are Adie, only this evening I was talking
about my friends.
Get me a knife

Adie

use your fingernails

Michel

I send these guys candles every week
Mr Popinou – he is the best friend of all

Adie

I can't get the tape off

Adie gets a knife out of his pocket.
They open the tape.

Michel

he used to send me gifts for you
when you were little

sweets or treats. They get things easier in the city.
He knew that children like sweets.

It is a parcel made from brown paper.

Michel
See, even the brown paper is better quality over there.
Maybe he has forgotten that you are grown up now.

They open it.

Michel
Or just sent sweets for the hell of it.

Out of the parcel come several candles.

Michel
Is there no note?

Adie looks.

Michel
Well what does he mean?
It can't just be these Adie there must be something else
in there.
These are my candles.
I sent them to him only a few days ago.
Doesn't he like them?
Was the wick stunted? Didn't they light properly?
There must be a note Adie, look properly.

Adie looks.

Michel
Maybe he wants a bigger order but he forgot to put
the note in.
He has had my candles every week for twenty years
Adie
I don't know what he means

Adie
there's nothing.

Adie shows Michel.

Adie

Maybe he can get them cheaper in the city

Michel

of course he can get them cheaper in the city
he can get any sort of candles and any sort of colour.
But he always said he liked mine.

Adie screws up the brown paper.
Pause.

Michel

Maybe I should ring him.
Ask him what he means? I have his telephone number
after all
Or walk to his door.
He can't have died
it's his writing on the parcel.
He has been my friend for twenty years.

Pause.
Adie stands up.
Beat.
Adie starts to walk off.
He stops.

Adie

It means don't send any more candles Dad.
That is what it means.

Michel

I know what it means.
You don't need to patronise me Adie
I know what it means.

Adie walks past.

SCENE FIVE

Next morning.
Sita is sitting curled up in the den.
She is asleep.
A noise wakes her up.
She opens her eyes.
She kind of sits up.
Another noise.
She jumps.

Sita
  Fuck sake

Sol
  you're a bit jumpy aren't you?

Sita
  yeah well I didn't know it was you.

Sol
  Calm down

Sita
  you bloody idiot

Sol
  you didn't used to mind

Sita
  yeah well I do now.

She stands up.

Sita
  What you doing here?

Sol
  Followed you.

Sita
  Where is Jean?

Sol shrugs.

Sita
I wish you'd stay away from him

Sol
you aren't his minder

Sita
he was better off before he got mixed up with you

Sol
he has his own mind to make up

Sita
unfortunately.
Let go.

Sol
Why?

Sita
I said let go.

Sol
I've got a hard on

Sita
Christ Sol

Sol
just a little kiss?

Sita
Get off me.

She fights him.
He fights back.
She knees him. He gets her by the hair.

Sol
Why should I?

Sita
because

Sol
yeah because?

Sita
Because if you don't I'll tell everyone it was you

Sol
that did what?

Sita
that skinned that bride.

He drops her.
He spits on her.

Sita
Well wasn't it?

He walks away.

Sol
Don't

Sita
you aren't even going to deny it.

Sol
You don't get it.

Sita
No I don't.

Jean walks in. He is carrying a box.
He whistles.

Jean
Fantastic.

Sol
Come on Jean we are going

Jean
just let me move the stuff in

Sita
you can't leave stuff here

Jean
well, who is going to stop us?

Sita
this place isn't yours

Jean
well if it isn't ours and it isn't yours we are both trespassers

Sita
take it away with you

Jean
just for a couple of days. This place isn't used.

He puts the box down.

Sita
What is in it?

Jean
well it isn't kittens I tell you that

Jean laughs.

Jean
it certainly isn't kittens

Sita
let me see

Jean
I wouldn't do that if I were you

Sita
chocolate

He laughs again.

Sita
let me see Jean

Jean
might regret it
might see something you wished you hadn't

Sol
chocolate was last year's game sweetheart

Jean
when we were babies

Sita
what is it?

Sol
he told you, none of your business

Jean
wouldn't get too near though

Sita
get off.

He pushes her too roughly.
She falls back.
Jean stands up and pretends to piss on her.
He laughs.

Sita
You are disgusting

Jean
says the freak queen
hey at least I have still got both my nipples

Sita
get off

Jean
let's have a look?

Sita

Get off.

He tries to undo her shirt.
She is trying to get out of his hold.

Sol

Get off her Jean

Jean gets off her.

Jean

she is my bloody sister

Sol

doesn't mean you can do what you want.

Sol comes over and slaps her.

Sol

Only I can do that.

He slaps her again.

Jean

Oi –

Sol slaps her a third time.

Jean

Sol –

Sol

You ever say anything again, I'll kill you.

He walks out.
Jean looks at Sita.

Jean

You okay yeah?

Sita

Why are you hanging out with him?

Jean
why not? you did

Sita
yeah well I made a mistake

Jean
god he is just a mate

Sita
yeah well don't lose all your others.

Sol comes back in.

Sol
You coming?

Jean goes.
Sita is left.
She goes to the cubby hole.
She takes out the gun.
She pretends to fire after them.
Michel comes in another way.
She turns around and aims it at him.
Pause.
He puts his hands up.

Michel
I'm looking for my son

Sita
no one here

Michel
I can see that
only I thought, he comes here sometimes

She puts her arm down.

Michel
Are you okay?
I'm sorry but you don't look like a assassin.

Sita
It doesn't work anyway

Michel looks at it.

Michel
it does
you just have to know how to load it

Sita
how do you load it?

Michel
I'm not telling.
You shouldn't have it

Sita
I thought it didn't work

Michel
yeah well.
Even a gun that doesn't work shouldn't be played
with.
Lots of kids come by here, that is why it shouldn't be
hanging about.

Michel puts his hands out.

Michel
give it to me

Sita goes towards him.

Sita
how do I know you won't blow my head off?

Michel
you don't
you only have my face to go by.

Sita
I am not good at reading faces
I always chose the bad ones.

Beat.

Sita
What will you do with it?

Michel
I will put it somewhere safe.
Somewhere it won't be found.

Sita
I've got fond of it

She puts it into his hand.
Michel puts it back in the cubby hole.

Michel
don't touch it again.

Beat.
Michel starts to go.

Michel
What's in the box?

Sita
kittens

Michel
oh
can I look?

Sita
no

Michel
they aren't making a noise

Sita
they are sleeping

Michel
oh
you are minding a box of sleeping kittens?

60

Sita
someone has to look after them

Michel
even when they are sleeping?

Beat.

Michel
anyway like I say, I was looking for my son but –

Sita
I'm looking for my boyfriend

Michel
I doubt they are the same person

Sita
we had a fight I said something I didn't mean

Beat.

Sita
we are going to get married

Michel
that is nice

Sita
set up a little home

Michel
here?

Sita
where else?

Michel
no one seems to like here any more

Sita
not me
I love it here

Michel
  so do I.

Sita
  Maybe I should marry you then?

Michel
  I am already married

Sita
  oh

Beat.

Michel
  are you sure you are okay?

Sita
  sure

Michel
  only . . .

Sita
  You don't need to worry about me
  you only just met me, I pulled a gun on you, what the
  hell you doing worrying about me?
  I am always alright.
  Anyway everyone always asks how I get by but it is
  like I have got a guardian angel or something

She takes a little icon out of her pocket.

Sita
  here

He looks at it.

Sita
  see
  she looks after me.
  Gets me into scrapes fair enough, but gets me out of
  them afterwards

Michel goes into his pocket.

Michel
me too

He shows her his icon.

Sita
yours is in better nick

Michel
not really

Sita
bet you polish yours

Michel
only with my thumb.
As I stand thinking, or praying. I run my thumb over it

Sita
never shown anyone mine before

Michel
I don't believe it

Sita
okay but never shown anyone old. A real person.

Beat.

Sita
I've seen you at the church

Michel
oh

Sita
I live there

Beat.

Sita
up at the top.

Where you can climb in summer.
I look down on the congregation

Michel
you can't live there

Sita
why not?

Michel
pigeons

Sita
I push them out.
Bung the little nests down.
They don't come back

Michel
don't you have a home?

Sita
it is my home

Beat.

Sita
listen this isn't one of these sorry tales. I do okay

Michel
guardian angel

Sita
yes

Michel
does the priest know?

Sita
the old one did, I don't know about the new guy

He doesn't say anything.
She puts hers back in her pocket.

Sita
你 you are a nice man

Michel
  thanks

Sita
  most men aren't

Michel
  that's not true

Beat.

Sita
  I'll see you

Michel
  okay

Sita
  can I kiss you?

Michel
  no

Sita
  see that is why you are nice.

She walks out.
Michel is left.

Michel
  what about the kittens?

She has gone.
He looks in the box.

Michel
  for the love of god.

He looks around.
He realises he should get the box out of there.
He drags the box off.

SCENE SIX

Michel brings the box into the house.
Therese comes down the stairs. She is still dressed in her
nightclothes.

Therese
  you should have woken me

Michel
  I wanted you to sleep

Therese
  it's late already

Michel
  a little sleep

She yawns.

Michel
  you called out in the night
  I didn't hear what you said
  I tried to wake you

Therese
  must have been a dream

Michel
  you were clutching your side

Beat.

Therese
  I feel fine.
  A little sleepy but . . .

Beat.

Michel
  are you ill Hannah?

Therese
Hannah?

Michel
Therese I meant Therese
I was thinking of Hannah but –

Therese
you were thinking of Hannah?

Michel
I . . .

Pause.

Michel
are you ill Therese?

Beat.

Therese
No.

Pause.

Therese
What is in there?

Pause.

Michel
candles

Therese
oh

Michel
new batch arrived
just raw wax but I can make them up into something

Therese
can I see?

Michel
no
sorry. They are a bit experimental I want to be sure of
them

Therese
okay.

Beat.

Michel
Thomas was here

Therese
I know

Beat.

Michel
he was sorry to miss you
he left you some doughnuts
I'll get them for you

She puts a hand up, as if to say no.

Michel
I think he puts too much salt in anyway these days
they have too much of everything over there
he is profligate, even with the salt

Therese
maybe.

Michel
I bet his raisin breads are the same

Beat.

Therese
we do tell each other the truth don't we?

Pause.

Michel
Of course we do.

Therese
I need to get up, I can't stay like this all day.
I have things to do.

Therese cries.

Michel
What is it?

Therese
We don't talk to each other

Michel
of course we do

Therese
we haven't told each other a single thing for years.

Pause.

Michel
The box isn't full of candles

Therese
I know that

Michel
it is full of explosives.

Therese
What are you doing with a box of explosives?

Michel
don't say it like that

Therese
why did you bring explosives into our house?

Beat.

Michel
I brought them here because I didn't know what to do
with them.
That is the truth.
You know what I am.
I would not bring a box of explosives into the house.

Beat.

Therese
I am sorry.

Michel goes and gets the box.
He opens it.

Michel
If you have an idea of what to do with it I wouldn't
mind the answer.

Therese
Where did it come from?

Michel
from a girl.
She said it was kittens

Therese
chuck it in the river

Michel
people drink from the river
kids play in the river

Therese
they would dissolve
float away

Michel
they would poison our water supply.

Therese
You can't keep them here.

One accident with the candles and the whole house
will go up.

Michel
Maybe I should take it to the priest.
He could talk to the congregation about the folly of
this sort of thing.
The congregation could pray over the box and hope it
turns into flour.
We could get Thomas to bake it into doughnuts.
Miracles happen. The mother of Christ, she has
appeared in breadsticks before.

Therese
Don't speak like that

Michel
why shouldn't I?
You don't believe in any of it any more.

Beat.

Therese
But you do.

Beat.

Michel
Do you want to move?

Pause.

Therese
I don't know.

Michel
The writing is on the wall, that is what Thomas said.

Beat.

Michel
you know the irony about explosives is that they make
them out of the same stuff that makes the soil sweet.

There is a noise.
Hannah comes in.

Hannah
I tried the door but you didn't hear
Adie is standing outside my house
he came to my door
he is in a mess

Michel
what do you mean?

Hannah
He has got blood all over his face

Therese
Adie?

Hannah
yes

Michel
it can't be Adie

Hannah
he looks like he has been in a fight.
I didn't ask him.
He can tell you himself.

Beat.

Hannah
Well aren't you coming?

Beat.

Michel
is he hurt?

Hannah
It's hard to tell, his face –

Therese
I'll go.

Hannah
   He needs someone to comfort him

Michel
   he shouldn't be fighting

Hannah
   kids fight
   he is just a kid

Therese
   Michel, I will go.

Beat. Therese looks to Michel for something.

Hannah
   So come then?
   You need his permission to come?

Beat.

Hannah
   All he needs is a parent.
   Someone to put their arms around him and say it is
   okay.

Beat.

Therese
   Michel?

Hannah
   Why do you keep looking at him?

Beat.

Hannah
   Do you need to give her permission?
   For God's sake Therese come and comfort your son.
   Michel?
   Forget it, by the time you get out there the cut will
   have healed up.

She storms out.
Pause.

Therese
It will be a school-yard fight.

Michel
Yes.
It will.

They don't move.

SCENE SEVEN

Adie being comforted by Hannah.

Hannah
Hold still.
It's just going to sting a bit more
you were lucky they didn't have your eye out.

Adie
it wasn't at school.

Hannah
Well you had better tell your dad it was.

Adie
I went over the bridge.

Hannah
You don't have to tell me

Adie
I . . .

Pause.

Hannah
go back into your house hmm?
Tell them what happened. Tell them it wasn't your
fault

74

Adie
I can't say that.
I'd fight again.

Hannah
Then you are a fool.

Adie
I went to an address.
One of Dad's friends. He sent back some candles

Hannah
you shouldn't have been there

Adie
I wanted to ask him why

Pause.

Hannah
you had better hold that against your face.
You'll have a black eye in the morning.

Adie
The son came out.
He just started shouting stuff at me.
He called me a bride-killer
I didn't kill the fucking bride

Hannah
don't swear Adie

Adie
Hannah

Hannah
I mean it, don't swear

Michel comes out.

Michel
how is he?

Hannah

he'll live.

he is cross more than anything

Michel

thanks Hannah.

Michel sits down next to him.
He take Adie's hand and kisses it.
Beat.
Michel kisses his hand again.

Adie

Mr Popinou spat when I said I was your son

Michel

come to church with me.

Hmm?

Let's go and see if we can find the priest. That is where to take this. Ours is the faith of the peacemaker. That is what he will say. When I was young I used to have prayers that I used to chant when I felt angry. I know there are injustices but you can't let them turn into your own anger. Not like this. You have to remember that. Whatever happens, you stay cool. You stay decent. You act out of love. We don't let ourselves get riled. They hate us, we pray, they kill us, we pray, they bulldoze our houses. We pray.

That is the only way we win.

Adie

They pray too

Michel

I know that

Adie

so how does that work?

Michel

they pray to a different God

76

Adie
they believe the same things

Michel
not about the host. It's different.
Our faith is founded on what we believe about the host

Adie
I don't care about the host

Michel
well you should. It cares about you.

Pause.

Adie
They are going to piss all over us Dad

Michel
that may be so

Adie
all my friends and their parents are leaving.
There are all these rumours about what is coming in
on the airfield
I don't know what we can do

Michel
we leave it up to the politicians
there have been crises like this before
it blows over

Adie
they hate us over there

Michel
if we don't fight we don't lose

Adie
it isn't about winning or losing
they will win anyway
it is just about not turning over and letting them.

Beat.

Michel
Will you come to church?

Beat.

Adie
Okay.

Michel
Thank you
thank you God
it is the only place to take it.

Adie
I'll come later

Michel
Thank you.

Adie picks up his coat.

Michel
You are our pride and joy Adie

Adie
I don't think you are right about everything by the way.

Michel
I am not saying you should.

He leaves.
Hannah and Michel watch.

Hannah
He was more hurt than he was letting on

Michel
we are all more hurt than we let on.

Beat.

Hannah
> You can't make your children see things the same way
> that you do
> you should know that Michel.

SCENE EIGHT

Sita is in the hideout.

Sita
> Who is that?

Adie
> only me

Adie comes in.

Adie
> Shushh
> don't say anything.

He comes up to her. He kisses her.
He strokes her face.
He takes his shirt off.
Underneath he has the wounds of someone who has been flogged.
She gives a sharp intake of breath.

Sita
> What did they do to you?

Adie
> shush.

He undoes her shirt.
They both have wounds now.
They kiss.

Act Two

SCENE ONE

Jean in the street. Where the women play dice.
Jean is kneeling down and drawing on the ground in chalk.
Adie comes along. He looks at it.
Jean keeps working.

Adie
It's just language

Jean
so?

Adie
language never changed anything

Jean
depends what it says.
I can write the same thing in eight languages
anyone of any nation walking by here could
understand

Adie
but no one walks by here

Jean
in the air then.
Them watching from the sky,
in their planes, their airships
even the fuckers from other countries who see what is
happening here on their news

Adie
what does it say in all these languages?

Jean
it says DIE YOU TOSSHEAD CUNTS

Beat.

Adie
  cool.

Adie reads it.
Jean snaps the chalk in half and gives it to him.
Adie puts his in his mouth and swallows it.

Jean
  What do you do that for?

Adie shrugs.
Jean carries on working.

Adie
  He isn't coming

Jean
  who?

Adie
  that guy you hang around with
  I saw him on the bridge

Jean
  what do you mean?

Adie
  go and look

Beat.

Jean
  what do you mean on the bridge?
  he's just late
  he has done this before

Adie
  you go and look then

Jean
  what would I see?

Adie
    I wouldn't like to describe it

Jean
    tell me what the fuck I would see?

Adie
    military vehicles on top
    soldiers
    and underneath
    a noose.
    And a body hanging.

Pause.

Jean
    I don't believe you

Adie
    go and see

Jean
    fucking bastards

Beat.

Jean
    fuck the fucking . . .
    you had better not be kidding.

Adie
    I wish I was.

Jean
    Shit

Beat.

Adie
    they have written underneath as well. It's one of your
    languages
    I didn't understand it.

Jean
Bastards.

Beat.

Adie
You okay?

Beat.

Jean
He did the bride.

Adie
I guessed
I guessed that is what it said

Beat.

Adie
but there must have been a reason,
Was there a reason?

Jean
Of course there was a reason
He did the bride because the bride's brother did his
sister.
And they did her worse

Beat.

Adie
how could they have done her worse?

Jean
she didn't die
not straight away

Beat.

Adie
so it was fair then

Jean
of course it was fair.

Beat.

Jean
Can I borrow your bike?
I want to go and see

Adie
you can't get across on a bike

Jean
can I borrow it or not?

Adie
you can borrow what you want

Jean
what else have you got?

Adie
Nothing much.

Beat.

Adie
I've got a girl

Jean
I know your girl

Adie
I've got a place

Jean
I know your place

Adie
I have got a weak mother and old-fashioned father

Jean
you've got an uncle

Adie
how do you know about my uncle?

Jean
I watched him drive right through the streets.

Adie
So I have got an uncle then.

Jean
So you have.

SCENE TWO

Thomas and Therese are in the house.
Thomas is looking around at the walls again.

Thomas
The pictures

Therese
icons

Thomas
do you need to have so many?

Therese
we like it

Thomas
all these faces looking at you

Therese
you get used to it

Thomas
they give me the creeps

Therese
they bring you luck

Beat.

Thomas
have they brought you luck?

Therese
they brought us Adie
we weren't supposed to be able to have children
remember

Thomas
I suppose they did.

Therese
Anyway home was the same

Thomas
not so many

Therese
just as many and mother would clean them every day
now at least I don't do that.

Beat.

Therese
Sorry I know you don't like her name to be spoken

Thomas
it's not as bad as that

Therese
you never even ask about her.

Beat.

Therese
What do you have on your walls in the city?

Beat.

Thomas
Cinema stars

Therese
still faces

Thomas
they have better bodies.

Therese laughs.
It hurts a little.

Therese
You shouldn't make me laugh.

Pause.

Thomas
Here
for you

Therese
I don't have a jug

Thomas
doesn't matter.

Therese takes the flowers.

Therese
Thanks.

Thomas
Are you happy?

Therese
I suppose so.

Beat.

Therese
Pass me that tin

He passes the tin.
She takes out some leaves.
She chews them.

Thomas
what is that for?

Therese
nothing. Habit probably.

Thomas sits down.
In front of him is a present.

Thomas
Are you going to open it?

Therese
flowers then a present?

Thomas
why shouldn't I spoil you?

Therese
shouldn't I wait for Michel to get back?

Thomas
up to you

She opens it.
Inside is a television.

Therese
oh.

Thomas
I know the electricity isn't good but I thought
on high days and holidays

Therese
thank you.

Thomas
You do know how to work it?

Therese
we aren't so backward, Thomas, honestly you make it
sound like we live in the last century.
Hannah has one.

Thomas
She would

Therese laughs.

Therese
    she has a good one

Thomas
    not as good as this.
    Do you want me to turn it on?

Therese
    later

Thomas
    you could watch a soap

Therese
    oh

Thomas
    you don't like soap?

Therese
    I don't know
    I haven't ever seen them
    Hannah watches them

Thomas
    does she like them?

Therese
    difficult to tell.
    You know Hannah.

Beat.

Thomas
    I have something else.

He goes into his bag.

Thomas
    But first I want to show you something.
    It isn't mine

I borrowed it
I shouldn't have it really
I certainly shouldn't show you

He takes out a map.

Thomas
I have a friend in the town hall

Therese
what is it?

He spreads it out.

Thomas
they have some of the dimensions wrong
I guess they are going by aerial photographs or
something

Therese
why are you showing me this?

Thomas
the area in blue
there is nothing
the area in green
that is where they intend to mine first

Therese
how do you know this?

Thomas
I told you I have a mate

Therese
but the church is in green

Thomas
I know.
And all the houses to the west. Your house.

Therese
They can't mine under the church.

He puts the map away.

Thomas
    You shouldn't have seen it.
    God Therese I don't know what I have to do to get
    you and Michel out of here

He gives her the bag.

Thomas
    gift number three
    money
    I've brought my car
    you can get in the car and I can get you all out of here
    we can drive to the train station
    you don't have to live with me, you can live anywhere

He shows her his bag.

Thomas
    you could take it, all of it.
    You could live anywhere you wanted in the world.
    You could go to another country even

Therese
    why would we want to go to another country?

Thomas
    I'm just saying
    anywhere, a different continent, I don't know
    somewhere less hot
    where do you fancy?

Pause.

Therese
    put away your money Thomas.

Thomas
    Therese please

Therese
    it is up to Michel

91

Thomas

for God's sake
when will you stop deferring everything to Michel?
There are already soldiers on the bridge.
If they block it, there is going to be no way out.
What the hell will it take to get you away from here?

Silence.

Therese

For you to have arrived just once and said you were
going to see her

Therese picks up the flowers.

Therese

that those were for her and not me
that would have surprised me, that would have been
enough

Beat.

Therese

What if I were to say she would have to come too?
What if that had been my condition Thomas, what
then? Then perhaps you would understand. The times
I pleaded with you, begged you to see her, just once
I said, but no. Now you know what it is like to be up
against an immovable mountain.
She is dead you ridiculous piece of childhood.
Already gone.
And yours was the only name in her addled state she
could remember.

Beat.

Therese

Yes cry now.

Thomas

When?

Therese
This time last year.
The longest day of the summer

Thomas
oh my God.

Beat.

Therese
I've been waiting until you asked
That was when I was going to tell you.
The first moment you spontaneously mentioned her name
she was an old woman Thomas.
How could you have been scared of an old woman?

Michel comes back in. Furious.
He sits down in silence.

Michel
And don't tell me he is young.
He is old enough to know better, he is at least thirty-two
Or whatever age he is, even at seventeen he should know something

Therese
Michel?

Thomas stands up.
Michel hardly even notices him.

Michel
The only consolation was Adie wasn't there.
The church Therese.
The church and I –

Therese
it can't be over

Michel

I left

And I will never walk in there again, as long as that man is preaching.

This is it Therese we are not members of that church any more.

Beat.

Michel

He has no measure

He doesn't know how to talk to the young.

The whole place is like a tinder box we don't need him to ignite us.

Rows of young men sitting at the front mouths open like fools, greedy for his bloodlust.

I stood up, I tried to stop him.

Me and a few of the other elders.

We must talk about communication I shouted, compromise

You can't use this loaded language.

So a young man has lost his life on the bridge, do we need to lose more?

Where does God talk about killing?

Where does God talk about compounding hatred with hatred?

A young man has been lynched, let's weep not kill.

You know what he did?

He said, how do you know what God would do?

Indeed, I said, but how do you?

He said new times needed new theology.

New theology, I asked, what do you mean, new theology?

That killing is right, that maiming is suddenly okay?

He asked me to leave.

Beat.

Is this what the church has come to preach Therese?
Have I missed something?
What new theology?
Weren't we the faith of the peacemakers?
WHAT NEW THEOLOGY?
God is the only thing we have to hang on to.
Does he mean to give us a new God too?

Pause.

Therese
Thomas gave me a television

Michel
is that all you can say?

Pause.
Thomas shakes his head.
He gets up to go.
Pause.

Thomas
I'll leave the bag

Michel
what is in it?
Therese what is in it?

Beat.

Thomas
Money

Michel
we don't want it

Therese
that is what I told him

Thomas
just in case,
Therese?

He lifts the bag and puts it at Therese's feet.

Michel
  Wait.
  I have a question for you.
  It's a funny thing, but it got my mind to wondering.
  How did you know about the mud? How did you
  know what they intend?
  How did you come by so much money selling bread?
  How come you can afford a luxury car?
  Hmm?
  You are a baker.

Thomas
  I have a friend

Michel
  we all have friends.
  Mine don't deal in mud.

Thomas
  I have nothing to do with it

Michel
  not what I heard

Thomas
  you are my family

Michel
  exactly.

Pause.

Thomas
  Therese
  It's not true.

Michel
  I think you should go

Thomas
  it isn't true.

96

Therese turns her head away.
Thomas leaves.
Michel picks up the television and lets it smash.
Therese stands up and gets a dustpan and brush.

Michel
    Just leave it.

She stops.
She cries.
He bends down to her.
He puts his arms around her.

Michel
    You talk about compromise.
    That is what. You go back to the old theology. The
    young will always be excited, you calm them down
    with parables, you read to them and you read to them
    and you read to them.
    They need wisdom that is all, not to be armed with
    rhetoric.

Thomas comes back in.

Thomas
    My car it –
    It's not there . . . it was there just a moment ago,
    it –

They both look at him.

Thomas
    How can I get home?
    I . . .

He leaves.
Michel rocks her like a baby.

Michel
    Shush.

SCENE THREE

Sita comes into the den.

Sita
Adie?
Adie I –

She stops. There is no one there.

Sita
Is this a game?
We . . .

She looks around.

Sita
I am not playing hide and seek with you.
You here or not?

She sees debris.
Old food cans.
Some wires.
And some wire-cutters.
She picks up a sheet of instructions.
She puts it down.

Sita
Shit.

SCENE FOUR

Michel is trying to fix the television.
Therese is asleep.
He has put some tape across the broken screen.
A small picture flickers into action.
It comes and then is gone.

Michel
　Damn.

Michel fiddles again.
Sita enters.

Sita
　Do you know where Adie is?

Michel stops, he looks at her.

Michel
　no

Sita
　it's important

Michel
　what is important?

Sita
　you should be keeping tabs on him

Michel
　he is fifteen

Sita
　you are his parents aren't you?

Michel is still involved with the television.

Michel
　yes

Sita
　well parents are supposed to do that, parents are
　supposed to know where their kids are. If you are a
　parent you have got to do more than just feed your
　kids. It's no good just watching them from afar and
　hoping for the best

Michel
　I'll bear it in mind

Sita
    I am serious

Beat.
Michel looks at her.
The TV flickers into life again.

Michel
    would you look at that

Sita
    are you going to talk to me?

Michel notices that Sita isn't leaving.
He turns the TV off.

Michel
    is there a problem?

Sita
    I don't know.
    There might be. Would it even bother you if there was?

Michel
    Of course.

Sita
    I think he has gone into town.

Michel
    well he is an idiot what can I say?

Sita
    this time I think they took a car

Michel
    they?

Sita
    he is with my brother.
    And you shouldn't let that comfort you by the way, my
    brother is no maiden aunt.

Michel

Can he drive?

Sita

I don't think that driving was the point.
They are moving stuff.
Don't ask me for more I'm only going on intuition.
I'm not his fucking parent am I?

Michel

What are you saying?

Sita

Have you still got that box?
The one I gave you.

Michel

Yes

Sita

thank god.
Where is it?

Michel

I hid it

Sita

well go and make sure it is where you left it.

Michel

He was studying for exams

Sita

it doesn't mean anything

Michel

we bought him a new textbook

Sita

So? A new fucking textbook doesn't make a character
does it?
You and me, we talked yeah
I wouldn't muck you about. I'm serious

Michel looks at her.

Michel
I'll go and check

Sita
now

Michel
okay.

Michel goes.
Sita is still in a state.

Sita
And hurry up.

She sees Therese sleeping.

Sita
Sorry.
Oh God it is you.

She looks at her.
She feels her forehead.
Michel comes back in.

Sita
Well?

Michel nods.

Michel
Nothing

Sita
You need to ring someone.
Do something
you could ring ahead warn someone
get on the phone

Michel
what would I say?

Sita

they were talking about the centre of town
I don't know.
They took a car, they could have filled it with that stuff.
You should warn someone.
If it turns out to be a false alarm they will only shout
halleluia, they won't shoot you. Everyone loves a false
alarm
and if it isn't, then . . .

Michel

Adie wouldn't know how to. To make a bomb you
need to know about physics

Sita

you can get that stuff from anywhere. You can plug a
computer into a telephone wire and they tell you.

Michel

I will make a call

Michel goes to the phone.
He picks up the receiver.
Therese stirs.

Michel

It's okay

Therese

Adie?

Sita

Hurry.
I am not pissing about.
When he got hurt he changed.
I'll swear on anything

Therese

what's going on?

Sita

Adie has taken a car

103

Michel
if this turns out to be a joke

Sita
no joke

He tries the phone.
Desperately tries to get through.

Sita
try again

Michel
it is a Monday
the damn thing should work

Therese
tell me what is going on?

Michel
it is a Monday isn't it?

Pause.

Therese
Michel?

Sita
it's a Tuesday

Michel
shit

Michel talks while still trying the phone.

Michel
Adie is out doing something.
We don't know what it is.

Sita
It's not going to be good?

Michel tries the phone again.

Therese
   what kind of not good

Sita
   shit not good
   fucking awful not good

Michel
   work, you blasted damned thing . . .

Therese
   what?

Sita
   I didn't think they would do it. They are usually so full
   of shit.

Michel
   It's a bloody Tuesday, it would be a bloody Tuesday.
   Why would it have to be a Tuesday?

Sita
   You got to get across that river and stop them

Michel
   it will take me hours

Sita
   take his bike
   I've got his bike outside

Michel
   why won't you go?

Sita
   because he is your son.

Michel looks at them both.

Sita
   why should I be here doing this, why should I give a
   fuck?

That is it, I have warned you now.
You do what the hell you like about it. Take the
fucking bike or bunny-jump I don't care.
I am not his flipping parent. And I'm not doing your
job for you.

She starts to go.

Michel
Wait
where exactly were they headed?

Sita
I don't know
There are soldiers on the bridge, you will have to lie
your way across

Beat.

Sita
the main square, that is where I would try first.

Michel starts to leave.

Sita
And next time, keep better bloody tabs on him.
Ground him or something, I don't know. Beat him up
if he even leaves the house. Why do you need me to
tell you?

Michel has gone.

Sita
You can't just let your kids be

Sita and Therese sit in silence for a second.

Sita
well you can't

Sita paces up and down.

Sita
he can ride a bike yeah, your old man?

Therese
yes

Sita
maybe I should have gone, I'd get past those soldiers
on the bridge

Therese
Adie is just a boy really

Sita
is that right?

Beat.

Therese
sit down you are making me nervous

Sita
you make me nervous

Therese
this is my home

Sita
you look like my mum did

Beat.

Therese
what do you mean?

Sita
she had what you've got

Therese
how do you know what I have got?

Sita
the lines on your face
says it all over

Therese
there is nothing wrong with me

Sita
not what your face says

Therese puts her hand up to her face.

Therese
what is it?

Sita
I don't know
But it killed her, and no doubt it will kill you.
You pissing blood yet?

Pause.

Sita
No skin off my nose, I was only asking

Therese
yes.
Yes I am

Sita
and when you vomit you feel like you can taste your
shit?

Therese (*faint*)
yes.

Sita
won't be long then, will it?

Beat.

Therese
I take wintergreen
it helps

Sita
that is what she did

Therese
I pray sometimes

Sita
she did that too

Pause.

Sita
listen I don't mean to be rude but I can't just wait here.
I've got to get down there, see what is going on.

Pause.

Sita
You take care, yeah?

She has gone.
Therese puts her hand back up to her face.

SCENE FIVE

Hannah is standing, trying to listen to a radio.
An aeroplane goes overhead.
She takes the headphones off in irritation.

Hannah
Shush.

It comes back.
She tries to re-tune.

Hannah
Oh for God's sake.
Just let me tune in would you?
just once.

SCENE SIX

Sita climbs into the den.
She sits all hunched up and waits.

SCENE SEVEN

Therese at home.
She is on the phone.
She is trying to get through.
She starts to feel ill.
She sits down and retches.

An explosion is heard.
They all hear it.

SCENE EIGHT

Hannah is still trying to tune in the radio.
Michel walks the bike in. He looks shattered.
She takes the headphones off her ears.
He looks at her.

Hannah
  No?

He closes his eyes.

Hannah
  Tell me it isn't true

He falls to the floor.

Hannah
  oh god no.

She approaches him.
He hangs on to her waist.
He cries.

Michel
  I can't go home
  I can't tell her
  she is waiting, I can't tell her

SCENE NINE

In the house.

Therese
Adie?
ADIE

SCENE TEN

Michel is still speaking to Hannah.

Hannah
How many?

Michel
Scores.
Scores and scores.
Children, mothers. Young men,
People going about their business
buying papers
eating sandwiches.
And Thomas, his own uncle, among the dead.
They chose the most busy place.
A two-year-old in a buggy. Head in two pieces.

Hannah gets down on the floor so she is at the same height as him.

Michel
how can I go home?
How can I tell her, he did this?

She takes out her handkerchief.
She wipes his eyes.

Michel
How can I?

He looks for the answers in Hannah's face.

Michel
    How can I?

SCENE ELEVEN

Jean at the base of the church tower.
He stands at the bottom and shouts up.

Jean
    Sita
    Sita

He pulls on a bell.

Jean
    Sita I know you are up there

The bell sounds.

Jean
    fucking come down you cunt

Sita
    piss off

Jean
    you don't know what happened

Sita
    I never want to see you again

Jean
    you have got to help me

No answer.
He rings the bell again.

Jean
    you have got to fucking help me

He is panicking.

Jean
Jesus Christ you have got to help me

He is sweating, wiping his armpits.
She drops something from on high.

Jean
Christ you bitch.
That fucking hit me.

She drops something else.

Jean
Just let me talk to you

She comes down.

Sita
is Adie dead?

Pause.

Sita
is Adie dead?

Jean
no
no he isn't.
They got him, but he isn't dead.

Sita
So you didn't even have the balls to be in the car

Jean
you have got to fucking help me.
You have got to say you saw me, they'll get me next
I had to swim the river to get back here

Sita
you killed a crowd of people

Jean
it wasn't supposed to be like that

Sita
how was it supposed to be?

Jean
the fucker who owned the car
he set it off
he wasn't supposed to be there
Adie said he was at home
he just turned up on a truck and set the whole thing
off.
please please Cee

Sita
fuck off

Jean
you are my bloody sister

Sita
I never want to see you again.

Jean
Just hold me –

Pause.

Jean
I . . .

He starts to cry.

Jean
I have never seen –
Shit it was –

He starts to shake.

Jean
I can't breathe, I . . .

She stands there and watches.
She spits on him.
She walks away.

Hannah and Therese on a patch of land next to a wood.
Therese is walking with a stick.
They walk in.
They look around.

Hannah
When I was a kid you could get a train from here that
would take you to anywhere.
Anywhere you wanted to go.

Therese looks around.

Hannah
Do you need to sit?

Therese
Not just yet.

Hannah puts up a travel-chair.

Hannah
For God's sake Therese.
Don't be a martyr.

Therese sits.
Hannah looks about.

Hannah
It is not so bad

Therese
it is a little windy

Hannah
hmm.
There isn't any mud

Therese
that is true.

Pause.

Hannah
I quite like it

Therese
do you?

Hannah
it is a change.
Your mother would have liked it.

Therese
No she wouldn't

Hannah
she might.

Therese
If she hadn't have died she'd be dead by now.
Once she had heard about Thomas
both on the same day in the year.
All three, you could say.

Hannah takes a handful of the soil.

Hannah
It's good soil
feel.
And you can pay them to put up a hut. You buy your
own land.
They put up a temporary house.
Who knows how long we will be here?

Therese
What will happen?
Hannah
What will happen next?

Hannah
You weren't supposed to ask today.
We are supposed to be getting you away from all that

Therese
I might not see him again.

Hannah looks up at the sky.

Hannah
Who knows

She goes into her bag.

Hannah
I have brought some cake
do you want some?

Therese
No

Hannah puts it away.

Therese
did we all go wrong somewhere?

Beat.

Therese
what has the longest day in the year got against me?

Beat.

Hannah
I know where they are holding him.
Him and others like him.
Do you want to know?

Therese
I . . .
Yes.

Hannah
On the other side of the airfield
If you go round the long way
the side that stares into the sun
there is a part they haven't built yet
and so they use it . . .

Therese nods.

Hannah
Michel could go and see him

Therese
he'd be shot

Hannah
you can get in.
If you walk round the right way
you can stand on the other side of the wire and talk

Therese
how do you know?

Hannah
I went.

Beat.

Hannah
I told you before, we all love Adie.

Therese
Are you saying you saw him?

Hannah
I didn't talk to him.
I just went to –
I don't know why I went.
Was that the wrong thing to do?

Therese
What did he look like?

Hannah
he looked tired
the sun was hot he looked hot
his hair seems to have grown a little

Therese
it was definitely him?

Hannah
yes.

Therese
Maybe I –

Hannah
it's too far.
Therese you can hardly . . .

Therese
I know.

Beat.

Hannah
What about Michel?
Would Michel go?

Therese
I don't know

Hannah
he could take something from you.

Therese
you are sure you can talk to them

Hannah
they don't seem to care
they look like caged animals.
Maybe Michel would go.

Pause.

Therese
Not if I asked him
He and I . . .
we have hardly said two words
he can't look me in the face, he . . .
I don't know what he is thinking, what he is doing.

Pause.

Therese
He is like a stranger.

Pause.

Hannah
We should go.
It's a fair way home.

Therese
You could ask him.

Beat.

Therese
He still loves you.

Hannah
Therese

Therese
he always has really

Beat.

Therese
it is okay.
I don't care.
But you could ask him.
Couldn't you?

Hannah nods.
An aeroplane goes overhead.

Hannah
Can you see? Through the trees

Therese
where?

Hannah
there.

They look.

Hannah
  So many now

Therese
  you would have thought they would have taken
  enough photographs
  you would have thought they have already mapped
  every scrap of land.

Hannah
  Not here.

Therese
  Let's hope not.

SCENE THIRTEEN

On the broken side of the airfield.
Jean behind barbed wire.
It is still hot.
Very hot. Jean is sort of hallucinating in the heat, talking
to imaginary men and women who surround him and
taunt him.

Jean
  Oi
  you got something to drink?
  Anything
  I . . .
  I'll drink your piss if you'll piss into a cup for me.

He mimes taking a cup from someone.

Jean
  Oh cheers mate.

He pretends to drink.

Jean

It burns
It's so long since I drank I –
What you been eating that makes your piss burn?
You been on some kind of drug?

Michel walks up.

Michel

I am looking for my son

Jean

you been watching me?

Michel

no

Jean

got anything to drink? Please I am so thirsty I could
die

Michel

they don't give you water?

Jean

they only give you enough to keep you alive.
The dogs drink the rest.
Piss for me? That would do

Michel

I can't piss I . . .

Jean

or shit then, that has moisture doesn't it
or slit your throat and I will drink your blood
I don't care really

Michel

maybe it will rain for you

Jean

do you think?

Michel
this heat when it breaks it could thunder

Beat.

Jean
that would be great
that would be flipping wonderful.
I would love that.
You aren't kidding me?
Because I haven't got much else to hang on to right now

Michel
no

Jean
fantastic

Michel
I have a stick of liquorice

Jean
okay

Michel gives it to him through the wire.
Jean eats it.

Jean
I hate the stuff.
Normally but this . . .

Michel
I'm looking for my son.

Beat.

Jean
And who is your son?

Michel
Adie.

Jean
Adie is dead.

123

Beat.

Michel
Oh

Jean
sorry

Michel
I wanted to give him some stuff from his mother

Jean
he died.
The thirst it got to him
the thirst and the heat and the beatings
the bastard couldn't survive the beatings
you had better give it to me instead.

Beat.

Michel
You sure, he . . .?

Adie walks up to the barbed wire.

Adie
Dad

Michel
Adie

Adie looks in a terrible way.
He falls to his knees on the other side of the barbed wire.

Jean
I asked him to piss for us
he wouldn't

Adie
how is Mum?

Michel
she is okay.

Beat.

Adie
Jean would you?

Jean
alright but if he gives you anything you share it with
me.

Jean walks away.

Michel
I only came here because
your mother, she . . .
you look terrible

Adie
I am okay

Michel
you look ten years older

Adie
my exams were today.
If I had been . . .

Michel
you would have passed

Adie
we don't know that

Michel
you would have got flying colours

Adie
maybe.

Beat.

Adie
We didn't know that the car would go off like that

Michel

    I don't want to hear about it

Adie

    it wasn't how it was supposed to go

Michel

    you have given them the perfect excuse.
    They are getting the bulldozers ready to move in.
    All they needed was a reason . . .
    And you gave it to them

Adie

    it wasn't how it was meant to be.

Pause.

Michel

    How was it meant to be?

Adie

    They killed a friend of Jean's
    they strung him up to the bridge

Michel puts his hand up, he doesn't want to hear any more.

Adie

    I am sorry Dad

Beat.

Michel

    your mother wanted me to –
    I have some stuff from her.

He takes out a little package.

Michel

    I don't know what she was thinking but anyway
    some cake

He hands it through the bars.

Michel
a bit of reading

Michel looks at the title.

Michel
it is a novel, I guess she reckons you would have a fair
amount of time on your hands.
A pencil, do you want a pencil?

Adie
I'll take it

Michel
and a pear.

He hands it through the bars.
Adie falls on the pear like someone who hasn't eaten for
a long time.
He eats the pear. Michel watches.

Michel
I have something else.
That was from your mother.
She and I, as you know, we differ on things.
Anyway.

He takes out another handkerchief.
He unwraps it.
Inside is the gun.

Michel
This is from me.

He holds it up to Adie.
Adie realises he is going to shoot him.

Michel
Ours was the faith of the peacemaker Adie.
Never trust a change of theology.

Adie
Please . . .

Michel shoots him.
He falls down dead.

Michel
    And now we are both murderers

He throws the gun down.
He walks away.

SCENE FOURTEEN

Hannah and Therese are putting things in boxes.
They are packing.

Hannah
    What about these?

She picks up a pile of icons.
Therese shakes her head.

Therese
    Michel may want them.

Hannah
    I doubt it.

Therese
    Habits die hard.

Therese reaches out for something. She is suddenly in a
lot of pain.
Hannah comes to her side.

Therese
    I am okay

Hannah
    I know you are

Therese
    just a little

Hannah
sure.

It passes.

Hannah
are you sure that life in a temporary hut is going to
suit you?

Therese
it won't be for long

Hannah
well that is the beauty of the word 'temporary'

Therese
no, the huts will become permanent
no one will rebuild them
we'll be there for generations
it's me that is temporary

Beat.

Hannah
don't be so fucking morbid
I am going to keep you alive for years.

Therese laughs a little.
It hurts again.

Hannah
What about the dice? Shall we take them?

Therese
How else shall we talk to each other?

Hannah
Very true.

Hannah puts them in her pocket.
Michel comes in.

Michel
It looks so different

Therese
it was always a dark house.
It was only our things that cheered it up.

Michel sees the icons.

Therese
Do you want them?

He looks through.

Michel
No.

Therese
I put some clothes out for you upstairs

Michel
thank you

Therese
I didn't know what . . .

Michel
I will see to it

Beat.

Therese
will you go and see him again?

Michel
I expect

Therese
how is he?

Michel
okay.

Therese
I am asking about my son Michel, how is he?

Beat.

Michel
　he is a little thirsty
　and a little dirty
　and a little beaten

Therese
　has he read the book?

Michel
　he loved it.
　He asked for another.

Hannah
　I told you he would like it.

Therese
　You will go again?

Michel
　Of course.
　I said already.

　Beat.

Michel
　How much more have you got to do?

Hannah
　We are done really, we were waiting for you
　we can't take much
　these huts, apparently there isn't much space.

Michel nods.

Therese
　You won't change your mind?

Michel
　no

Therese nods.

Therese
　well it is goodbye then.

She stands up.
Hannah comes to her side.

Michel
Will you manage the walk to the coach?

Hannah
I will carry her if I have to.

Michel and Therese kiss.

Therese
I have all this money Michel
all of Thomas's money
no don't look like that
I want you to spend it on a lawyer
I want you to do everything you can for Adie
it's in an envelope on the table

Michel
what about you?

Therese
you know that I won't make much longer
you have to look after him now.

Therese kisses him again.

Therese
and thank you.
I enjoyed it. All these years

Michel
some of it

Therese
we did okay.

Michel
We did okay.

Therese
  It is funny isn't it, when it comes to it, there is so little
  to say.

Beat.
Therese starts to walk out.

Hannah
  Bye

Michel
  Bye.

They have gone.
Michel goes to the window and watches them go.
He looks around.
He goes to the table.
He looks at the money.
He puts it down.
He goes to the icons.
He looks through.
He puts them back around the place.
He doesn't like their glaring faces, suddenly they seem
like too much.
He turns them to face the wall.
Sita comes in.
She watches him.

Sita
  You can still have mine

She hands her little icon to him.

Sita
  I am sorry about everything.

Michel
  You haven't gone?
  You should get out of here
  get on the coach

Sita shakes her head.

Sita
no

Michel
you have a chance of another life
you are young.
Go

Sita
I don't want to.

Michel
I can give you some money

Sita
I don't want money

Michel
they are coming in with bulldozers
and mine blasts

Sita
I know

Michel
they won't be watching out for people in the way

Sita
I wondered if you wanted to come up to the church?
You said you always wanted to go to the top.
You could see what there is from the top

Michel
they will go for the church first

Sita
I know.

Beat.

Michel
You are too young.

Sita
And you are too old.

She puts out her hand.

Michel
It will turn into nation against nation.
Already there is international outcry, other armies will
arrive. What started as a small settlement fighting its
neighbour will attract other parties like flies to . . .
Lots of people will die.

Sita
You would like the view
from the top.
I know you would

Beat.

Michel
would I?

Sita
certainly

Michel
it's a long way to climb if I don't.

He takes her hand.